The Breakfast Club: 50 Recipes to Energize Your Morning

By: Kelly Johnson

Table of Contents

- Avocado Toast with Poached Egg
- Banana Oat Pancakes
- Greek Yogurt Parfait with Granola
- Spinach and Mushroom Scramble
- Overnight Chia Pudding
- Sweet Potato Hash with Eggs
- Blueberry Almond Smoothie
- Classic French Toast
- Breakfast Burrito with Salsa
- Cottage Cheese and Fresh Fruit Bowl
- Protein-Packed Smoothie Bowl
- Scrambled Eggs with Smoked Salmon
- Coconut Banana Bread
- Whole Wheat Waffles with Berries
- Veggie Breakfast Quesadilla
- Classic Breakfast Burrito
- Zucchini Frittata
- Apple Cinnamon Oatmeal
- Smoked Salmon Bagel with Cream Cheese
- Tofu Scramble with Veggies
- Peanut Butter and Banana Smoothie
- Sweet Cornmeal Pancakes
- Chocolate Chip Banana Muffins
- Avocado and Tomato Breakfast Salad
- Smashed Chickpea Toast
- Chia Seed Granola Bars
- Ham and Cheese Croissant Sandwich
- Almond Butter and Banana Smoothie
- Porridge with Maple Syrup and Walnuts
- Breakfast Tacos with Scrambled Eggs
- Quinoa Breakfast Bowl
- Egg and Spinach Breakfast Wrap
- Mango Coconut Smoothie
- Poached Eggs with Sautéed Kale
- Blueberry Chia Jam on Toast

- Oatmeal with Berries and Almonds
- Egg Muffins with Vegetables
- Avocado Smoothie
- Bacon and Egg Breakfast Cups
- Cinnamon Apple Quinoa Bowl
- Breakfast Sandwich with Avocado
- Pumpkin Spice Smoothie
- Cucumber and Cream Cheese Sandwich
- Breakfast Polenta with Tomato and Egg
- Grilled Peach and Ricotta Toast
- Tofu and Avocado Breakfast Wrap
- Sourdough Toast with Almond Butter
- Protein Pancakes with Berries
- Carrot Cake Oatmeal
- Roasted Tomato and Basil Frittata

Avocado Toast with Poached Egg

Ingredients:

- 1 ripe avocado
- 2 slices whole-grain bread
- 2 eggs
- Salt and pepper to taste
- Red pepper flakes (optional)
- Fresh lemon juice (optional)

Instructions:

1. Toast the bread slices until golden brown.
2. While the bread is toasting, bring a small pot of water to a simmer. Crack each egg into a small bowl and gently slide into the simmering water, cooking for about 4 minutes until the whites are set but the yolk is runny.
3. Mash the avocado in a bowl and season with salt, pepper, and a squeeze of lemon juice.
4. Spread the mashed avocado on the toasted bread.
5. Top each slice with a poached egg and season with salt, pepper, and red pepper flakes if desired.

Banana Oat Pancakes

Ingredients:

- 1 ripe banana, mashed
- 1 cup rolled oats
- 1/2 cup milk (dairy or non-dairy)
- 1 egg
- 1 teaspoon vanilla extract
- 1/2 teaspoon baking powder
- 1/4 teaspoon cinnamon
- Pinch of salt
- Butter or oil for cooking

Instructions:

1. In a blender, blend the oats until they form a fine flour-like texture.
2. Add the mashed banana, milk, egg, vanilla extract, baking powder, cinnamon, and salt to the blender and blend until smooth.
3. Heat a non-stick skillet over medium heat and add a small amount of butter or oil.
4. Pour 1/4 cup of the pancake batter onto the skillet and cook for 2-3 minutes on each side, or until golden brown.
5. Serve with maple syrup or your favorite toppings.

Greek Yogurt Parfait with Granola

Ingredients:

- 1 cup Greek yogurt
- 1/4 cup granola
- 1/4 cup mixed berries (blueberries, strawberries, raspberries)
- Honey (optional)
- Chia seeds (optional)

Instructions:

1. Layer Greek yogurt in a glass or bowl.
2. Top with granola and berries.
3. Drizzle with honey and sprinkle with chia seeds if desired.
4. Serve immediately as a quick and nutritious breakfast.

Spinach and Mushroom Scramble

Ingredients:

- 2 eggs
- 1/2 cup fresh spinach, chopped
- 1/4 cup mushrooms, sliced
- 1 tablespoon olive oil or butter
- Salt and pepper to taste

Instructions:

1. Heat olive oil or butter in a skillet over medium heat.
2. Add the mushrooms and cook for 3-4 minutes, until softened.
3. Add the spinach and cook until wilted.
4. In a small bowl, whisk the eggs with salt and pepper.
5. Pour the eggs into the skillet with the vegetables and scramble until cooked through.
6. Serve warm, garnished with additional salt and pepper if desired.

Overnight Chia Pudding

Ingredients:

- 2 tablespoons chia seeds
- 1/2 cup milk (dairy or non-dairy)
- 1/2 teaspoon vanilla extract
- 1 teaspoon honey or maple syrup (optional)
- Fresh berries or fruit for topping

Instructions:

1. In a jar or container, combine chia seeds, milk, vanilla extract, and sweetener if using.
2. Stir well and cover the container.
3. Refrigerate overnight, or for at least 4 hours, until the chia seeds have absorbed the liquid and the pudding has thickened.
4. Top with fresh berries or fruit before serving.

Sweet Potato Hash with Eggs

Ingredients:

- 1 medium sweet potato, peeled and diced
- 1/2 bell pepper, chopped
- 1/4 onion, chopped
- 2 eggs
- 1 tablespoon olive oil
- Salt and pepper to taste

Instructions:

1. Heat olive oil in a skillet over medium heat.
2. Add the diced sweet potato and cook for 8-10 minutes, stirring occasionally, until tender.
3. Add the bell pepper and onion, and cook for an additional 5 minutes until softened.
4. In a separate pan, fry or scramble the eggs to your liking.
5. Serve the sweet potato hash topped with eggs, and season with salt and pepper.

Blueberry Almond Smoothie

Ingredients:

- 1/2 cup frozen blueberries
- 1/2 banana
- 1/4 cup almond butter
- 1 cup almond milk
- 1 tablespoon honey (optional)
- Ice cubes (optional)

Instructions:

1. Combine the blueberries, banana, almond butter, almond milk, and honey in a blender.
2. Blend until smooth.
3. If you want a colder smoothie, add a few ice cubes and blend again.
4. Pour into a glass and enjoy.

Classic French Toast

Ingredients:

- 2 slices of bread (thick, such as brioche or challah)
- 1 egg
- 1/4 cup milk
- 1/2 teaspoon cinnamon
- 1/4 teaspoon vanilla extract
- Butter for cooking
- Maple syrup for serving

Instructions:

1. In a bowl, whisk together the egg, milk, cinnamon, and vanilla extract.
2. Heat a skillet over medium heat and add butter.
3. Dip each slice of bread into the egg mixture, coating both sides.
4. Cook the bread in the skillet for 2-3 minutes on each side, until golden brown.
5. Serve with maple syrup and your favorite toppings.

Breakfast Burrito with Salsa

Ingredients:

- 2 eggs
- 1/4 cup shredded cheese
- 1/4 cup salsa
- 1 flour tortilla
- 1/4 avocado, sliced
- Salt and pepper to taste

Instructions:

1. In a skillet, scramble the eggs over medium heat until cooked through.
2. Remove from heat and stir in the shredded cheese until melted.
3. Warm the flour tortilla in the skillet for about 30 seconds on each side.
4. Fill the tortilla with scrambled eggs, salsa, and avocado slices.
5. Roll up the tortilla, folding in the edges, and serve immediately.

Cottage Cheese and Fresh Fruit Bowl

Ingredients:

- 1 cup cottage cheese
- 1/2 cup mixed fresh fruit (berries, banana slices, mango, etc.)
- 1 tablespoon honey or maple syrup (optional)
- 1 tablespoon chia seeds or flaxseeds (optional)

Instructions:

1. Spoon the cottage cheese into a bowl.
2. Top with your choice of fresh fruit.
3. Drizzle with honey or maple syrup if desired.
4. Sprinkle with chia seeds or flaxseeds for added nutrition.
5. Serve immediately and enjoy!

Protein-Packed Smoothie Bowl

Ingredients:

- 1 frozen banana
- 1/2 cup Greek yogurt
- 1/2 cup almond milk (or any milk of choice)
- 1 tablespoon peanut butter or almond butter
- 1/4 cup protein powder (optional)
- Toppings: granola, sliced fruit, chia seeds, coconut flakes

Instructions:

1. Blend the frozen banana, Greek yogurt, almond milk, peanut butter, and protein powder (if using) until smooth and creamy.
2. Pour the smoothie into a bowl.
3. Top with your favorite toppings like granola, sliced fruit, chia seeds, and coconut flakes.
4. Enjoy immediately!

Scrambled Eggs with Smoked Salmon

Ingredients:

- 2 eggs
- 1 tablespoon milk or cream
- 1/4 cup smoked salmon, chopped
- 1 tablespoon butter or olive oil
- Salt and pepper to taste
- Fresh chives for garnish (optional)

Instructions:

1. Whisk the eggs with the milk or cream and season with salt and pepper.
2. Heat butter or olive oil in a non-stick skillet over medium heat.
3. Pour in the egg mixture and cook, stirring gently until the eggs are scrambled and soft.
4. Fold in the smoked salmon and cook for an additional minute.
5. Garnish with fresh chives if desired, and serve immediately.

Coconut Banana Bread

Ingredients:

- 1 1/2 cups whole wheat flour
- 1/2 cup shredded coconut
- 1 teaspoon baking soda
- 1/4 teaspoon salt
- 2 ripe bananas, mashed
- 1/4 cup honey or maple syrup
- 1/4 cup coconut oil, melted
- 2 eggs
- 1 teaspoon vanilla extract

Instructions:

1. Preheat the oven to 350°F (175°C). Grease a loaf pan.
2. In a large bowl, mix the flour, shredded coconut, baking soda, and salt.
3. In another bowl, combine the mashed bananas, honey or maple syrup, melted coconut oil, eggs, and vanilla extract.
4. Add the wet ingredients to the dry ingredients and stir until just combined.
5. Pour the batter into the prepared loaf pan.
6. Bake for 45-50 minutes, or until a toothpick comes out clean.
7. Let cool before slicing and serving.

Whole Wheat Waffles with Berries

Ingredients:

- 1 1/2 cups whole wheat flour
- 2 teaspoons baking powder
- 1/4 teaspoon salt
- 1 tablespoon sugar (optional)
- 1 1/4 cups milk
- 2 eggs
- 1/4 cup melted butter or oil
- 1 teaspoon vanilla extract
- 1/2 cup fresh berries (blueberries, strawberries, raspberries)

Instructions:

1. Preheat your waffle iron according to its instructions.
2. In a large bowl, whisk together the flour, baking powder, salt, and sugar.
3. In another bowl, whisk together the milk, eggs, melted butter or oil, and vanilla extract.
4. Pour the wet ingredients into the dry ingredients and stir until just combined.
5. Grease the waffle iron and pour in the batter, cooking according to your waffle iron's instructions.
6. Serve the waffles topped with fresh berries and a drizzle of maple syrup.

Veggie Breakfast Quesadilla

Ingredients:

- 1 whole wheat tortilla
- 2 eggs, scrambled
- 1/4 cup bell peppers, diced
- 1/4 cup onion, diced
- 1/4 cup spinach, chopped
- 1/4 cup shredded cheese (cheddar or your favorite cheese)
- Salt and pepper to taste
- Olive oil or butter for cooking

Instructions:

1. Heat a small amount of olive oil or butter in a skillet over medium heat.
2. Add the diced bell peppers, onion, and spinach. Cook for 3-4 minutes until softened.
3. Add the scrambled eggs and cook until fully set.
4. Remove the egg mixture from the skillet and set aside.
5. In the same skillet, place the tortilla and sprinkle with cheese.
6. Add the egg and veggie mixture on top, then fold the tortilla in half.
7. Cook for 2-3 minutes on each side until golden brown and the cheese is melted.
8. Serve immediately with salsa or avocado.

Classic Breakfast Burrito

Ingredients:

- 2 eggs, scrambled
- 1/4 cup black beans, drained and rinsed
- 1/4 cup shredded cheese (cheddar or your favorite cheese)
- 1/4 cup salsa
- 1 large flour tortilla
- Avocado slices for topping

Instructions:

1. Scramble the eggs in a skillet over medium heat until fully cooked.
2. Warm the tortilla in the skillet for 30 seconds on each side.
3. Lay the scrambled eggs, black beans, shredded cheese, and salsa in the center of the tortilla.
4. Fold in the sides and roll up the burrito.
5. Top with avocado slices and serve immediately.

Zucchini Frittata

Ingredients:

- 2 medium zucchinis, grated
- 6 eggs
- 1/4 cup milk
- 1/4 cup grated cheese (parmesan, mozzarella, or your choice)
- 1 tablespoon olive oil
- Salt and pepper to taste
- Fresh herbs for garnish (optional)

Instructions:

1. Preheat the oven to 375°F (190°C).
2. Heat olive oil in a large oven-safe skillet over medium heat.
3. Add the grated zucchini and sauté for 5 minutes, until tender.
4. In a bowl, whisk the eggs with milk, cheese, salt, and pepper.
5. Pour the egg mixture over the zucchini in the skillet.
6. Transfer the skillet to the oven and bake for 10-12 minutes, or until the eggs are set and slightly golden.
7. Garnish with fresh herbs and serve warm.

Apple Cinnamon Oatmeal

Ingredients:

- 1 cup rolled oats
- 2 cups milk (or water)
- 1 apple, diced
- 1 teaspoon cinnamon
- 1 tablespoon honey or maple syrup (optional)
- Chopped nuts or dried fruit for topping (optional)

Instructions:

1. In a pot, bring the milk (or water) to a boil.
2. Add the oats and reduce the heat to a simmer. Cook for 5-7 minutes, stirring occasionally.
3. Add the diced apple and cinnamon to the oatmeal.
4. Continue cooking for another 3-4 minutes, until the apple is tender.
5. Drizzle with honey or maple syrup if desired, and top with chopped nuts or dried fruit.

Smoked Salmon Bagel with Cream Cheese

Ingredients:

- 1 whole grain or plain bagel, halved
- 2 tablespoons cream cheese
- 2 ounces smoked salmon
- 1/4 red onion, thinly sliced
- Fresh dill for garnish
- Lemon wedges

Instructions:

1. Toast the bagel halves until golden brown.
2. Spread a layer of cream cheese on each half.
3. Top with smoked salmon, red onion slices, and a sprinkle of fresh dill.
4. Serve with a lemon wedge on the side to squeeze over the salmon.
5. Enjoy immediately!

Tofu Scramble with Veggies

Ingredients:

- 1 block firm tofu, drained and crumbled
- 1/4 cup bell peppers, diced
- 1/4 cup onions, diced
- 1/4 cup spinach, chopped
- 1 tablespoon olive oil
- 1 teaspoon turmeric
- Salt and pepper to taste
- Fresh herbs (optional)

Instructions:

1. Heat olive oil in a skillet over medium heat.
2. Add the diced bell peppers, onions, and spinach. Sauté for 3-4 minutes until softened.
3. Add the crumbled tofu to the skillet and cook, stirring occasionally for 5-7 minutes.
4. Sprinkle in turmeric, salt, and pepper, stirring to combine.
5. Cook until the tofu is golden and heated through.
6. Garnish with fresh herbs and serve immediately.

Peanut Butter and Banana Smoothie

Ingredients:

- 1 banana
- 1 tablespoon peanut butter
- 1/2 cup almond milk (or milk of choice)
- 1/4 cup Greek yogurt
- 1 teaspoon honey or maple syrup (optional)
- Ice cubes (optional)

Instructions:

1. Place all ingredients (banana, peanut butter, almond milk, Greek yogurt, and honey) into a blender.
2. Blend until smooth and creamy.
3. Add ice cubes for a colder smoothie, if desired.
4. Serve immediately in a glass and enjoy!

Sweet Cornmeal Pancakes

Ingredients:

- 1 cup cornmeal
- 1 cup all-purpose flour
- 2 tablespoons sugar
- 2 teaspoons baking powder
- 1/2 teaspoon salt
- 1 1/4 cups milk
- 2 eggs
- 2 tablespoons butter, melted
- 1 teaspoon vanilla extract

Instructions:

1. In a large bowl, whisk together the cornmeal, flour, sugar, baking powder, and salt.
2. In a separate bowl, whisk together the milk, eggs, melted butter, and vanilla.
3. Pour the wet ingredients into the dry ingredients and stir until just combined.
4. Heat a skillet or griddle over medium heat and lightly grease.
5. Pour 1/4 cup of batter onto the skillet and cook until bubbles form on the surface. Flip and cook for an additional 1-2 minutes until golden brown.
6. Serve with butter, syrup, or fresh fruit.

Chocolate Chip Banana Muffins

Ingredients:

- 1 1/2 cups all-purpose flour
- 1 teaspoon baking soda
- 1/2 teaspoon salt
- 2 ripe bananas, mashed
- 1/4 cup sugar
- 1/4 cup brown sugar
- 1/2 cup vegetable oil
- 1 large egg
- 1 teaspoon vanilla extract
- 1/2 cup mini chocolate chips

Instructions:

1. Preheat the oven to 350°F (175°C) and line a muffin tin with paper liners.
2. In a medium bowl, whisk together the flour, baking soda, and salt.
3. In a large bowl, mash the bananas. Stir in the sugar, brown sugar, vegetable oil, egg, and vanilla.
4. Gradually add the dry ingredients to the wet mixture and stir until just combined.
5. Fold in the chocolate chips.
6. Spoon the batter into the muffin tin, filling each cup about 2/3 full.
7. Bake for 18-20 minutes, or until a toothpick comes out clean.
8. Let cool before serving.

Avocado and Tomato Breakfast Salad

Ingredients:

- 1 avocado, diced
- 1 cup cherry tomatoes, halved
- 1/4 cucumber, sliced
- 1/4 red onion, thinly sliced
- 1 tablespoon olive oil
- 1 tablespoon balsamic vinegar
- Salt and pepper to taste
- Fresh basil leaves for garnish

Instructions:

1. In a large bowl, combine the avocado, cherry tomatoes, cucumber, and red onion.
2. Drizzle with olive oil and balsamic vinegar.
3. Toss gently to combine, being careful not to mash the avocado.
4. Season with salt and pepper to taste.
5. Garnish with fresh basil leaves and serve immediately.

Smashed Chickpea Toast

Ingredients:

- 1/2 cup cooked chickpeas, mashed
- 1 tablespoon olive oil
- 1 teaspoon lemon juice
- Salt and pepper to taste
- 1 slice whole grain bread, toasted
- Red pepper flakes (optional)

Instructions:

1. In a bowl, mash the chickpeas with a fork or potato masher until chunky.
2. Stir in the olive oil, lemon juice, salt, and pepper.
3. Spread the chickpea mixture over the toasted bread.
4. Sprinkle with red pepper flakes, if desired.
5. Serve immediately as a healthy, savory breakfast option.

Chia Seed Granola Bars

Ingredients:

- 1 cup rolled oats
- 1/4 cup chia seeds
- 1/4 cup honey or maple syrup
- 1/4 cup peanut butter or almond butter
- 1/2 teaspoon vanilla extract
- 1/4 cup dried fruit (raisins, cranberries, etc.)
- 1/4 cup chocolate chips (optional)

Instructions:

1. Preheat the oven to 350°F (175°C) and line a baking dish with parchment paper.
2. In a large bowl, combine the oats, chia seeds, dried fruit, and chocolate chips (if using).
3. In a small saucepan, heat the honey (or maple syrup) and peanut butter over low heat until melted and smooth.
4. Stir in the vanilla extract.
5. Pour the wet ingredients over the dry ingredients and mix until well combined.
6. Press the mixture into the prepared baking dish.
7. Bake for 15-20 minutes, until golden brown.
8. Let cool, then cut into bars. Enjoy as a grab-and-go breakfast or snack!

Ham and Cheese Croissant Sandwich

Ingredients:

- 1 croissant, sliced in half
- 2 slices ham
- 2 slices cheese (Swiss or cheddar)
- 1 tablespoon Dijon mustard (optional)
- 1 teaspoon butter (for toasting)

Instructions:

1. Preheat a skillet over medium heat.
2. Spread a thin layer of Dijon mustard on the bottom half of the croissant.
3. Layer the ham and cheese slices on the bottom half of the croissant.
4. Top with the other half of the croissant.
5. Butter the outside of the croissant sandwich and place it in the skillet.
6. Toast on both sides until golden brown and the cheese is melted, about 3-4 minutes per side.
7. Serve immediately and enjoy the warm, melty sandwich!

Almond Butter and Banana Smoothie

Ingredients:

- 1 banana
- 1 tablespoon almond butter
- 1/2 cup almond milk (or milk of choice)
- 1/2 cup Greek yogurt
- 1/2 teaspoon cinnamon (optional)
- Ice cubes (optional)

Instructions:

1. Place all ingredients (banana, almond butter, almond milk, Greek yogurt, and cinnamon) into a blender.
2. Blend until smooth and creamy.
3. Add ice cubes for a colder smoothie, if desired.
4. Pour into a glass and serve immediately!

Porridge with Maple Syrup and Walnuts

Ingredients:

- 1/2 cup rolled oats
- 1 cup milk (or water for a lighter version)
- 1 tablespoon maple syrup
- 2 tablespoons walnuts, chopped
- Pinch of salt
- 1/4 teaspoon cinnamon (optional)

Instructions:

1. In a saucepan, combine the oats, milk (or water), and a pinch of salt.
2. Bring to a simmer over medium heat, stirring occasionally.
3. Once the oats are soft and the porridge is thickened (about 5-7 minutes), remove from heat.
4. Stir in the maple syrup and cinnamon (if using).
5. Top with chopped walnuts and serve warm.

Breakfast Tacos with Scrambled Eggs

Ingredients:

- 2 small flour tortillas
- 2 eggs
- 1 tablespoon milk
- Salt and pepper to taste
- 1/4 cup shredded cheese (cheddar or Mexican blend)
- Salsa (optional)
- 1/4 avocado, sliced (optional)
- Fresh cilantro for garnish

Instructions:

1. In a bowl, whisk together the eggs, milk, salt, and pepper.
2. Heat a non-stick skillet over medium heat and lightly grease.
3. Pour the egg mixture into the skillet and cook, stirring occasionally until scrambled and cooked through.
4. Warm the tortillas in a separate pan or microwave.
5. Divide the scrambled eggs between the tortillas and top with shredded cheese, salsa, avocado slices, and cilantro.
6. Fold the tortillas and serve immediately.

Quinoa Breakfast Bowl

Ingredients:

- 1/2 cup cooked quinoa
- 1/4 cup Greek yogurt
- 1 tablespoon honey
- 1/4 cup mixed berries (blueberries, strawberries, raspberries)
- 1 tablespoon chia seeds
- 1 tablespoon sliced almonds

Instructions:

1. In a bowl, layer the cooked quinoa, Greek yogurt, and honey.
2. Top with fresh berries, chia seeds, and sliced almonds.
3. Mix together and enjoy a filling and nutritious breakfast bowl.

Egg and Spinach Breakfast Wrap

Ingredients:

- 1 large egg
- 1/4 cup spinach, chopped
- 1 whole wheat wrap
- 1 tablespoon cheese (optional)
- Salt and pepper to taste
- 1 teaspoon olive oil or butter

Instructions:

1. Heat olive oil or butter in a skillet over medium heat.
2. Add the spinach and sauté for 2-3 minutes until wilted.
3. Crack the egg into the skillet and scramble with the spinach until fully cooked. Season with salt and pepper.
4. Place the egg and spinach mixture onto the center of the wrap.
5. Sprinkle with cheese, if desired.
6. Roll the wrap tightly and serve immediately.

Mango Coconut Smoothie

Ingredients:

- 1 ripe mango, peeled and chopped
- 1/2 cup coconut milk
- 1/4 cup Greek yogurt
- 1 tablespoon honey or agave syrup
- Ice cubes (optional)

Instructions:

1. Combine the mango, coconut milk, Greek yogurt, and honey in a blender.
2. Blend until smooth.
3. Add ice cubes for a colder smoothie if desired.
4. Pour into a glass and serve immediately!

Poached Eggs with Sautéed Kale

Ingredients:

- 2 eggs
- 1 cup kale, chopped
- 1 tablespoon olive oil
- 1 clove garlic, minced
- Salt and pepper to taste
- 1 teaspoon vinegar (for poaching)

Instructions:

1. In a small saucepan, bring water and vinegar to a gentle simmer over medium heat.
2. Crack the eggs into individual small cups and carefully slide them into the simmering water. Poach for 3-4 minutes until the whites are set but the yolks are still runny.
3. While the eggs are poaching, heat olive oil in a skillet over medium heat.
4. Add garlic and sauté for 1 minute, then add the chopped kale. Cook until wilted, about 3-4 minutes.
5. Season with salt and pepper.
6. Plate the sautéed kale and top with the poached eggs. Serve immediately.

Blueberry Chia Jam on Toast

Ingredients:

- 1/2 cup fresh or frozen blueberries
- 1 tablespoon chia seeds
- 1 tablespoon honey or maple syrup
- 2 slices whole-grain bread
- Butter or coconut oil for toasting (optional)

Instructions:

1. In a small saucepan, cook the blueberries over medium heat, stirring occasionally, until they start to break down (about 5 minutes).
2. Stir in chia seeds and honey/maple syrup. Simmer for another 5 minutes until the jam thickens.
3. Toast the slices of bread in a toaster or on a skillet with butter or coconut oil, if desired.
4. Spread the blueberry chia jam on the toast and serve immediately.

Oatmeal with Berries and Almonds

Ingredients:

- 1/2 cup rolled oats
- 1 cup water or milk (or milk substitute)
- 1/4 cup mixed berries (strawberries, blueberries, raspberries)
- 1 tablespoon sliced almonds
- 1 teaspoon honey or maple syrup (optional)
- Pinch of cinnamon (optional)

Instructions:

1. In a small saucepan, bring the water or milk to a boil.
2. Add the rolled oats and reduce the heat to low. Cook, stirring occasionally, until the oats have absorbed the liquid and become tender, about 5-7 minutes.
3. Pour the oatmeal into a bowl and top with mixed berries, sliced almonds, and a drizzle of honey or maple syrup, if desired.
4. Sprinkle with cinnamon for extra flavor. Serve immediately.

Egg Muffins with Vegetables

Ingredients:

- 6 large eggs
- 1/2 cup bell pepper, diced
- 1/4 cup spinach, chopped
- 1/4 cup onion, diced
- 1/4 cup shredded cheese (optional)
- Salt and pepper to taste
- Cooking spray or oil for greasing the muffin tin

Instructions:

1. Preheat your oven to 350°F (175°C) and grease a muffin tin with cooking spray or oil.
2. In a bowl, whisk the eggs and season with salt and pepper.
3. Stir in the diced bell pepper, spinach, onion, and cheese (if using).
4. Pour the egg mixture evenly into the muffin tin, filling each cup about three-quarters full.
5. Bake for 15-20 minutes, or until the eggs are set and lightly golden.
6. Allow to cool for a few minutes before serving.

Avocado Smoothie

Ingredients:

- 1 ripe avocado
- 1/2 cup almond milk (or milk of choice)
- 1/2 cup Greek yogurt
- 1 tablespoon honey or maple syrup
- 1/2 teaspoon vanilla extract (optional)
- Ice cubes (optional)

Instructions:

1. In a blender, combine the avocado, almond milk, Greek yogurt, honey, and vanilla extract.
2. Add ice cubes for a colder smoothie, if desired.
3. Blend until smooth and creamy.
4. Pour into a glass and serve immediately!

Bacon and Egg Breakfast Cups

Ingredients:

- 4 slices bacon
- 4 large eggs
- Salt and pepper to taste
- 1/4 cup shredded cheese (optional)
- Fresh herbs for garnish (optional)

Instructions:

1. Preheat your oven to 375°F (190°C) and grease a muffin tin with cooking spray or oil.
2. Place a slice of bacon in each muffin tin cup, forming a "bowl" with the bacon.
3. Crack an egg into each bacon-lined cup.
4. Season with salt and pepper, and sprinkle with shredded cheese if desired.
5. Bake for 12-15 minutes, or until the eggs are set to your desired consistency.
6. Garnish with fresh herbs and serve immediately.

Cinnamon Apple Quinoa Bowl

Ingredients:

- 1/2 cup cooked quinoa
- 1/2 apple, diced
- 1/4 teaspoon cinnamon
- 1 tablespoon honey or maple syrup
- 1/4 cup almond milk (or milk of choice)
- 1 tablespoon chopped nuts (optional)

Instructions:

1. In a saucepan, heat the quinoa and almond milk over medium heat.
2. Stir in the diced apple and cinnamon.
3. Cook until the apple softens slightly, about 2-3 minutes.
4. Remove from heat and drizzle with honey or maple syrup.
5. Top with chopped nuts for added crunch, and serve warm.

Breakfast Sandwich with Avocado

Ingredients:

- 2 slices whole-grain bread
- 1 egg
- 1/4 avocado, sliced
- 1 slice cheese (optional)
- 1 tablespoon mayonnaise or mustard (optional)
- Salt and pepper to taste
- Butter for toasting (optional)

Instructions:

1. Toast the bread slices in a toaster or on a skillet with a bit of butter if desired.
2. In a pan, cook the egg to your liking (fried, scrambled, or poached).
3. Assemble the sandwich by spreading mayonnaise or mustard on one slice of bread, if using.
4. Top with the cooked egg, sliced avocado, and a slice of cheese (if using).
5. Season with salt and pepper, and close the sandwich with the other slice of bread.
6. Serve immediately and enjoy!

Pumpkin Spice Smoothie

Ingredients:

- 1/2 cup canned pumpkin puree
- 1/2 cup almond milk (or milk of choice)
- 1/2 banana
- 1/4 teaspoon pumpkin pie spice
- 1 tablespoon maple syrup
- 1/2 teaspoon vanilla extract (optional)
- Ice cubes (optional)

Instructions:

1. In a blender, combine the pumpkin puree, almond milk, banana, pumpkin pie spice, maple syrup, and vanilla extract.
2. Add ice cubes for a colder smoothie, if desired.
3. Blend until smooth and creamy.
4. Pour into a glass and serve immediately!

Cucumber and Cream Cheese Sandwich

Ingredients:

- 2 slices whole-grain or white bread
- 2 tablespoons cream cheese, softened
- 1/2 cucumber, thinly sliced
- Salt and pepper to taste
- Fresh dill or parsley for garnish (optional)

Instructions:

1. Spread the cream cheese evenly on one side of each bread slice.
2. Layer the thin cucumber slices on one slice of bread.
3. Season with salt and pepper, and top with fresh dill or parsley if desired.
4. Close the sandwich, cut in half, and serve immediately.

Breakfast Polenta with Tomato and Egg

Ingredients:

- 1/2 cup polenta
- 2 cups water or vegetable broth
- 1 tablespoon olive oil
- 2 large eggs
- 1/2 cup cherry tomatoes, halved
- Fresh basil leaves, chopped
- Salt and pepper to taste
- Grated Parmesan cheese (optional)

Instructions:

1. In a medium saucepan, bring the water or broth to a boil.
2. Slowly add the polenta while stirring to prevent lumps.
3. Reduce the heat to low and cook the polenta, stirring occasionally, for about 10 minutes, until thickened.
4. In a separate pan, heat olive oil over medium heat. Add the cherry tomatoes and cook for 2-3 minutes until softened.
5. Crack the eggs into the pan and cook to your desired doneness (fried, scrambled, or poached).
6. Serve the polenta in a bowl, top with the cooked tomatoes, eggs, and fresh basil. Sprinkle with Parmesan if desired. Serve immediately.

Grilled Peach and Ricotta Toast

Ingredients:

- 2 slices sourdough bread
- 1 ripe peach, sliced
- 1/4 cup ricotta cheese
- 1 teaspoon honey
- Fresh mint or basil for garnish (optional)
- Olive oil for brushing

Instructions:

1. Preheat a grill pan or outdoor grill.
2. Brush the peach slices and bread with olive oil. Grill the peaches for 2-3 minutes per side, until grill marks appear and they soften.
3. Toast the bread slices until golden and crispy.
4. Spread the ricotta cheese on the toasted bread.
5. Top with the grilled peach slices, drizzle with honey, and garnish with fresh mint or basil. Serve immediately.

Tofu and Avocado Breakfast Wrap

Ingredients:

- 1/2 block firm tofu, crumbled
- 1/2 avocado, sliced
- 1 small tomato, diced
- 1/4 cup spinach, chopped
- 1 whole wheat tortilla
- 1 tablespoon olive oil
- Salt and pepper to taste
- Hot sauce or salsa (optional)

Instructions:

1. In a skillet, heat olive oil over medium heat. Add the crumbled tofu and sauté for 5-7 minutes until slightly golden. Season with salt and pepper.
2. Add the chopped spinach and cook for an additional 1-2 minutes until wilted.
3. Remove from heat and place the tofu and spinach mixture in the center of the tortilla.
4. Top with sliced avocado and diced tomato. Add hot sauce or salsa if desired.
5. Roll up the tortilla, folding in the sides as you go, and slice in half. Serve immediately.

Sourdough Toast with Almond Butter

Ingredients:

- 2 slices sourdough bread
- 2 tablespoons almond butter
- 1 tablespoon honey (optional)
- Sliced banana or berries for topping (optional)

Instructions:

1. Toast the sourdough bread slices until golden and crispy.
2. Spread almond butter generously on each slice.
3. Drizzle with honey for extra sweetness, if desired.
4. Top with sliced banana or fresh berries for added texture and flavor. Serve immediately.

Protein Pancakes with Berries

Ingredients:

- 1/2 cup oats
- 1/4 cup protein powder (vanilla or unflavored)
- 1/2 cup egg whites
- 1/4 cup milk (or milk substitute)
- 1 teaspoon baking powder
- 1/4 teaspoon cinnamon
- 1/2 cup mixed berries (strawberries, blueberries, raspberries)
- Maple syrup or honey for serving

Instructions:

1. In a blender, combine the oats, protein powder, egg whites, milk, baking powder, and cinnamon. Blend until smooth.
2. Heat a non-stick skillet or griddle over medium heat and lightly grease with cooking spray.
3. Pour the batter onto the skillet, forming small pancakes. Cook for 2-3 minutes on each side, until golden brown.
4. Serve the pancakes with mixed berries and a drizzle of maple syrup or honey. Serve immediately.

Carrot Cake Oatmeal

Ingredients:

- 1/2 cup rolled oats
- 1 cup milk (or milk substitute)
- 1/2 cup grated carrots
- 1/4 teaspoon cinnamon
- 1/4 teaspoon nutmeg
- 1 tablespoon raisins (optional)
- 1 tablespoon chopped walnuts (optional)
- Maple syrup or honey (optional)

Instructions:

1. In a saucepan, bring the milk to a simmer over medium heat.
2. Add the oats, grated carrots, cinnamon, and nutmeg. Stir to combine and cook for 5-7 minutes, until the oats are tender.
3. Stir in raisins and walnuts, if using.
4. Drizzle with maple syrup or honey, if desired. Serve immediately.

Roasted Tomato and Basil Frittata

Ingredients:

- 6 large eggs
- 1/2 cup cherry tomatoes, halved
- 1/4 cup fresh basil, chopped
- 1/4 cup shredded mozzarella cheese (optional)
- 1 tablespoon olive oil
- Salt and pepper to taste

Instructions:

1. Preheat your oven to 375°F (190°C).
2. In a skillet, heat olive oil over medium heat. Add the cherry tomatoes and cook for 2-3 minutes until softened.
3. In a bowl, whisk the eggs and season with salt and pepper.
4. Pour the eggs into the skillet over the tomatoes. Sprinkle with fresh basil and mozzarella cheese, if using.
5. Transfer the skillet to the oven and bake for 10-12 minutes, until the eggs are set and lightly golden.
6. Slice and serve warm.

www.ingramcontent.com/pod-product-compliance
Lightning Source LLC
LaVergne TN
LVHW081508060526
838201LV00056BA/3004